IMAGES
of England

AROUND
LUTTERWORTH
THE SECOND SELECTION

A quiet Church Street scene. In the distance is the demolition of Kimpton Smith's shop, now the site of the town centre car park.

IMAGES
of England

AROUND
LUTTERWORTH
THE SECOND SELECTION

Geoff Smith

TEMPUS

Postcard, 1950s, published by L. Jones & Sons, Church Street, Lutterworth.

First published 2002
Copyright © Geoff Smith, 2002

Tempus Publishing Limited
The Mill, Brimscombe Port,
Stroud, Gloucestershire, GL5 2QG

ISBN 0 7524 2480 7

Typesetting and origination by
Tempus Publishing Limited
Printed in Great Britain by
Midway Colour Print, Wiltshire

Contents

A map of Lutterworth and villages featured in this book.

Introduction

After the success of the first volume, *Around Lutterworth*, I was asked to put together a further edition. This volume has several different villages featured and shows the area in some unusual and rarely seen photographs.

In the process of compiling this edition I have been very pleased to have been stopped in the street, telephoned and contacted by many of the locals of the area, who have often said, pop round for a cuppa and I will show you my old photographs, some of which I have included.

Thank you to the people who have helped with the two books and also for the people who look after the history of the area, helping with the museum, in local history groups, or just showing an interest. This keeps our history alive and kicking and brings people together from all walks of life from all over the world.

This compilation is a mixture of town and village changes through demolition of old, and construction of new buildings, past events and people, spanning two centuries.

Where possible names have been included with group photographs. This is an important point as many people have old photographs of family, friends and workmates with no names attached, and it will make such a difference for future generations if they can put a face to a family member or local person from long ago.

I would like to share with you several snippets taken from Bottrills Almanacks during the 1920s which readers may find of interest. They show one person's view of the changes in the town in which he lived and illustrate how we now take some things for granted which were then very precious. They were written by Mr Tom J. Laws, Scout leader and local character.

1923

'I said the last 12 months had been uneventful, yet one extraordinary event occurred which deserves chronicling. There was no marble season at the Elementary School! In all my many years experience I have never known such a thing. As a rule, marbles come out every springtime, but this year, alas, they were displaced by Fag cards. The glory has departed from Schoolboy Tradition – What may this ominous portent mean?'

1924

'I am not aware that this year has wrought any changes in the little town. The old names are still displayed over the same old shops, The market still consists of, at most, half-a-dozen stalls, the Narrows are as narrow as ever, New Street is still under water after every shower, Leicester Road as dark as pitch on a moonless night, There are still cobblestone pavements to break or strain ankles, cripple feet, hurt children who fall, and wear out boots – and the weird town hall still stands where it did!'
[I take it that Tom was not very happy with the town's situation at that time!]

1925

'Wireless's everywhere – I begin to think it will soon be a penal offence to be without it. It is certainly very wonderful. No need to worry if the clock is right now – you can sit in your own house and hear Big Ben chime 100 miles away. If it is a wet evening and you don't feel inclined to turn out for church or chapel, the singing of a first class choir, and the sermon of some great preacher, sounds in your ear at your own fireside. Opera's, plays, songs, music of all sorts, political and other speeches, the latest news, are now at a man's disposal for a very small outlay. The only drawback is that one cannot see as well as hear, but probably that will come soon. Fancy a working man sitting in his kitchen and witnessing a Lord Mayor's Banquet – the sight would properly send him frantically rushing out for a couple of faggots to have a banquet of his own. The visible stage of wireless is largely a matter of fancy yet.'

1926
'The past year has seen Lutterworth disturbed by a series of earthquakes. Street after street has upheaved, and pedestrians have been halted by sudden and surprising yawning gaps in the road and sidewalks for electric lighting has come to Lutterworth, and a great improvement it is, though it has left the paths in a very uneven state. May it soon be taken down Leicester Road which is still in darkness on winter nights.'

1927
'The new School in Woodmarket built by Mr Peter Rourke has been opened. As a matter of fact it was opened too soon, for there were no seats for the scholars for the first day or two, so it was opened again, formally a week or two later.'

It's very nice to know that all of the above has changed for the better, but it is good sometimes to see what people thought of the town they lived in...

As the museum is trying desperately to gain new, larger premises, profits from the sale of this book are to be donated to the Lutterworth Museum Building Fund.

The museum is open: Monday, Thursday, Friday, and Saturday: 10.00 a.m. until 4.00 p.m. March-October or by arrangement.

Acknowledgements

I would like to thank the people of Lutterworth and surrounding villages for putting up with me while compiling this book. A special thank you to my wife Alison and all of the people who have helped me or allowed photographs to be published: Mr and Mrs D. Mason, Mr J. Morris, Miss M. Petcher, Mrs E. Birch, Mrs S. Williams, Mr G. Holmes, Mr S. Smith, Carolyn and Lynn Jones, and Hector Marchant and family.

Map drawn by Mr A. Ainslow, Mr Robin Jenkins, The Records Office for Leicestershire, Leicester & Rutland, Lutterworth Museum.

Thank you to Mrs W. Warren of Vanished Views, South Kilworth. Copies of the photographs marked 'Vanished Views' can be purchased from Mrs Warren. Contact the museum for further information.

One
Bitteswell

The Nook, an ivy-covered cottage, *c.* 1900. Ivy proved to be a magnet for the glut of sparrows in the area at the end of the nineteenth century to the extent that it became a major problem. In response a sparrow society was formed and each parish was paid for the number of sparrows caught at 3d per dozen. Bitteswell claimed for 222 sparrows in the first 6 months of 1898.

The supply store. Mr Stanley Smith ran this store for many years taking over from his father in 1945. The shop first opened in 1919.

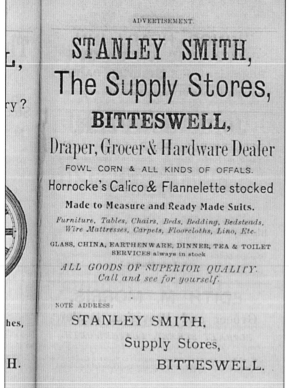

Smith's Stores, from *Bottrill's Almanack* 1923. This advertisement shows the wide range of goods available from the shop.

The school. Bitteswell has had three different schools. The first one was founded by a bequest in the will of Revd James Powell in 1844, the second school was built by public subscription in 1871, this is now the village hall. Finally the current school pictured here was built and opened in 1888. This building has been extended since the time of this photograph.

'Brewsters'. This wonderful three-storey house stands in its own grounds along the Ashby Lane.

CRICKET

"HOUNSFIELD" CHARITY CUP COMPETITION.

FINAL TIE.

COUNTESTHORPE BAPTISTS
v.
BITTESWELL

TO BE PLAYED AT
DUNTON BASSETT,
ON
TUESDAY, JULY 20, 1937
PLAY COMMENCES AT 7 P.M.

ADMISSION, 3d. - - School Boys, Free.

Ammon Bird, Printer, 1 Reg   st & 19a Market Place, Rugby.

Bitteswell Manor. The house came up for sale in 1936, after the death of the owner, for £2,500. The sale catalogue tells us that the house had a lounge, hall and cloakroom, four reception rooms, six bedrooms, two dressing rooms, a bathroom and ample maids' accommodation. The census of 1881 has six servants in residence. The house was demolished soon after the sale and was replaced with the current house that stands on the site.

Cricket poster.

Two
Broughton Astley

R MILL LANE AND PRIMETHORPE

Soar Mill Lane. The Soar Mill, situated about half a mile from here, was a water mill with a 13ft diameter wheel. The mill ceased working as a water mill in 1934, and was then used for the manufacture of tyres during the Second World War followed by a hosiery business. It is now a very popular hotel.

The Chestnuts, *c.* 1904. This house still stands but several houses have been built in what were once spacious grounds to the property with a swimming pool and tennis courts.

Mill Lane cottages, *c.* 1905. The thatched cottages had to be demolished after a fire in the early part of the last century.

Frank Hall's Cycle Stores, a very important shop in the village as cycling became one of the main forms of transport in the early 1900s.

Primethorpe. The Bulls Head public house is situated at the crossroads. Local builder, Frank Cooke owned the house on the left.

Broughton Astley Home Guard. This 1940's group was pictured on what is now the car park of the White Horse public house. From left to right, back row: Mrs Howe, -?-, -?-, -?-, -?-, -?-, -?-, Billy Hunt, -?-, Jack Pawley, -?-. Middle row: -?-, -?-, Arthur McCartney, -?-, -?-, -?-, Len Pickering, -?-, P.C. Oliver Lockton. Front Row: Cyril Pickering, Harry Hayler, -?-, Frank Bodicote, -?-.

Cricket club, 1931 division winners. From left to right, back row: Alf Hubbard, Horace Ford, George Brett, Sid Fretter, Dudley Cook, Bert Dawson, Ernie Hall, Phil Cooke, Arthur Pawley, Billy Hunt, Frank Brown. Middle row: Horace Starmer, Osro White, George Turner, Bille Rowe, Sid Mallard, Arthur Turner, Jack Mallard, Harry Burdett, Cyril Bailey, Charles Cooke, Ernie Harryman. Front row: Len Fretter, Wilf Andrews, Albert Pawley, Eric Fretter, Alf Brett, Frank Bodycote, Percy Turner, Horace Fretter, Tom Bennett, Bernard Nicholls, Arthur Nicholls, Stan Nicholls.

Three
Cosby

Cosby Views, *c.* 1902. This multi-view type card was very popular, giving people an insight into village life through four photographs. The top right photograph shows the Bulls Head Public House, bottom right is the Nook.

Main Street, *c.* 1903. The cottages in the centre of the picture were demolished and replaced by the church Sunday school building in 1920. The Huntsman Public House now stands on the left.

St Michaels church bells, 1914. The new bell second from the left is being hung along with the other bells. The church underwent major restoration by H. Cayley in 1907 and some re-fitting by F.J.F. Goodacre in 1909-1910. Another bell has been added subsequently.

Cottages in Brook Street. The wall of the churchyard adjoins the workers' cottages on the right hand side. On the left are three small bridges to give the house owners access to their property over the brook.

Village pageant, 1910. The children are dressed up as the old woman who lived in a shoe. Stuck to the wheels of the cart are advertising brochures.

Back Lane, now known as Park Lane. Looking from the Whetstone end of the village to the building in front, which is now the Co-op.

The Nook. This view from the early 1900s is from the point where Main Street crosses the brook. The thatched cottage, now demolished, has been replaced with the butcher's shop.

Four
Cotesbach

Main Street. This was also the location of the village shop and was a very important part of village life. This street scene now looks like an idyllic film set.

Cotesbach village. Cottages at the older part of the village are looking rather rundown.

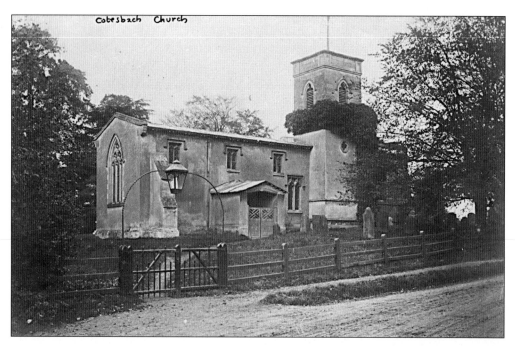

St Mary's church. A very unusual style of church, with fourteenth-century windows and a tower dating from 1812; this has been extensively worked on over the years. (Vanished Views)

The post office. Pictured outside the business they ran for many years are Eleanor Robinson (seated) and John Robinson.

Cotesbach Hall. Built as the rectory in the early eighteenth century.

The Church's Work of Spreading the Gospel in the British Empire Overseas and other parts of the World.

THE ANNUAL RURI-DECANAL

SALE OF WORK

For the above object, will be held

In the Garden at Cotesbach Rectory,

ON

SATURDAY, JUNE 14, 1924.

There will be a

SHORT SERVICE IN THE CHURCH

At 3 p.m., after which

MRS. MARRIOTT (COTESBACH HALL),

Has kindly consented to Open the Sale.

THE REV. A. E. BURNE

(Diocesan Organising Secretary for S.P.G.) will give a SHORT ADDRESS.

During the Afternoon and Evening

Two Missionary Plays

Will be given by the MEMBERS OF THE COTESBACH GIRLS' CLUB.

There will be TENNIS, CLOCK GOLF and other Competitions, &c.

Gifts of any kind (including Provisions and Live Stock), will be gratefully received by Mrs. Hindley and Mrs. Browne, Lutterworth; Mrs. Lloyd and Mrs. Tanner, Ashby Magna; Mrs. Machin, Broughton Astley; Mrs. Farrie, Cotesbach; Mrs. Metcalfe, Frolesworth; Miss Cox, North Kilworth; Mrs. Bryant and Mrs. Hill, South Kilworth; Mrs. Olver and Mrs. Saunders, Claybrooke; Mrs. Harris and Mrs. Starey, Sharnford; Mrs. Runnels-Moss, Shawell; Miss Mosse, Sapcote; Mrs. McMillan, Bitteswell; Mrs. Lloyd, Gilmorton; Mrs. Tanner, Bruntingthorpe; Mrs. Rogerson, Swinford; Mrs. Taylor, Mowsley; Mrs. Young, Kimcote; Mrs. Crosthwaite, Catthorpe; Mrs. Wright, Misterton; Mrs. Whitworth, Dunton Bassett; Mrs. Kimpton, Leire.

Admission, 6d. (Children under 12 Half-price).   After 5 o'clock, 3d.
Tea, 1/-.

C. W. COX, W. G. MOSSE, E. C. SYMES, H. J. TANNER,
HON. SECS.

J. E. Woodford, Printer, &c., High Street, Lutterworth.

Sale of work poster from 1924.

Five
Dunton Bassett

Children on a roundabout. This very early photograph, possibly from the 1860s, shows the Twigden family who started a fair with this hand-wound roundabout and were the first people who took rides to the Goose Fair in Nottingham. (Vanished Views)

Dunton Bassett School, 1936. From left to right, back row: Joseph Robinson (head teacher 1907-1946), Bob Dunkley, Phil Westwood, Maurice Swinfen, Maurice Brooks, John Carter, George Carter, Alan Swinfen, Fred Giles, Alan Boat, Mrs Johnson. Fourth row: Doris Fowkes, Elsie Kilpack, Cicely Crane, Audrey Brookes, Jean Fowkes, Betty ?, Kath Dore, Hilda York, Dorothy Judkins, Alberta Masters, Beatrice York, -?-, Cicely Kilpack, Brenda Asher, Peg Ellson, Pat Bryan. Third row: Geoff Mathews, Jill Webb, Margery Swinfen, Margaret Burman, Betty Asher, Jean Smith, Marion Taylor, Jean Ellson, -?-, Janet Gibbins, Barbara Bird. Second row: Vic Hammond, Les York, -?-, Giles, -?-, Giles, Peter Herring, Edwin Clarke, Malcolm Asher, Dennis Judd, Tony Bates. Front row: Derek Ellson, Leslie Fowkes, Margaret Fowkes, -?-, Wills, -?-, Wills, Phyllis Fowkes, Barbara Bates, Ted Smith.

Hill House. The post office, pictured on the right, has been in four different locations within the village over the last 100 years. It is now in Birmingham House opposite the former Crooked Billet Inn. (Vanished Views)

Crooked Billet. This was a public house for many years but is now a private residence. In this picture the pub is advertising 'Phillips & Marriott' Gold Medal Ales and Stout. Many of the original mullioned windows survive in the building today. (Vanished Views)

Needhams Cycles advertisement from *Abbotts Almanack*, 1929.

The Mount. Seen from the side of the village hall looking towards the centre of the village. Note the cobbled path and road gutter. (Vanished Views)

Main Street. A view looking north with a horse standing outside Birmingham House. (Vanished Views)

Six
Gilmorton

Horse and cart. This vehicle was standing in what is now the car park of the Red Lion public house.

Red Lion, Gilmorton. Built in the 1820s, Thomas Warden was the licensed victualler and maltster in 1870, while Joseph Glover ran the pub. From 1875-1884 Cornelius Earp was landlord, then in 1898 Eady & Dulley of Market Harborough paid £4,000 for the Red Lion and the Royal at Broughton Astley.

Crown Inn, school and post office. The school with its bell tower is now part of the Crown Inn.

School group. From left to right, back row: Henry Davies, -?-, -?-, -?-, Tom Bennett, -?-, Arthur Matthews, -?-, -?-. Middle row: -?-, Annie Measures, -?-, Kathleen Anderton, Rene Kingham, Peggie Green, -?-, -?-, Albert Smith. Front row: Mabel Boulter, May Broughton, Nora Broughton, Marie Kettell, May Green, -?-, Mr Moores.

School group. From left to right, back row: -?-, -?-, -?-, Arthur Broughton, Frank Broughton, -?-, Bill Green, George Woodward, John Woodward, -?-. Middle row: Miss Wormleighton, -?-, Thirza Matthews, Margaret Wolfe, Violet Bailey, Lily Green, -?-, Janet Chandler, Ethel Walton, -?-, Mona Gilliver. Front Row: -?-, -?-, -?-.

Advertisment for The Crown Inn and White Lion from *Abbotts Almanack*, 1912.

Gilmorton Mill. An unusual photograph, which shows the sails on the windmill. This building has now been turned into residential accommodation. The mills were a very important part of the lives of the people in the towns and villages. Over the years Broughton Astley and Cosby have also had windmills; Lutterworth has had three and a water mill.

THE MILL GILMORTON

M.C.P.L

Seven
Leire

Leire village. A little boy, dressed in his Sunday best, tends to the horse while the rest of the village looks deserted. Wormleighton of Leire who kept the drapers and fancy goods store in the village published this photograph.

Eaglesfield Farm. This advertising card was used by the proprietor of the farm to reply to customers' enquiries. The reverse has been printed with a standard reply.

Main Street, c. 1905. The group pose for their picture which was then made into a postcard and sold by John Abbott of Lutterworth.

Leire village. One hundred years later, apart from the cobbles there are not many changes to this scene. St Peter's school, which opened in 1873 and closed in 1947, is now missing its bell tower and chimney.

St Peter's church. This is a cabinet photograph, of a drawing, by C. Yardley, Royal Photographic Studio, Lutterworth and dates from approximately 1870. The church, with the exception of the tower, was completely re-built in 1867 at a cost of £2,000.

A tin-roofed cottage. This building is next to the Queens Arms public house and has latterly been thoroughly renovated.

Leire village 1887. People went to a lot of trouble decorating the village for Queen Victoria's Golden Jubilee.

Eight
Lutterworth

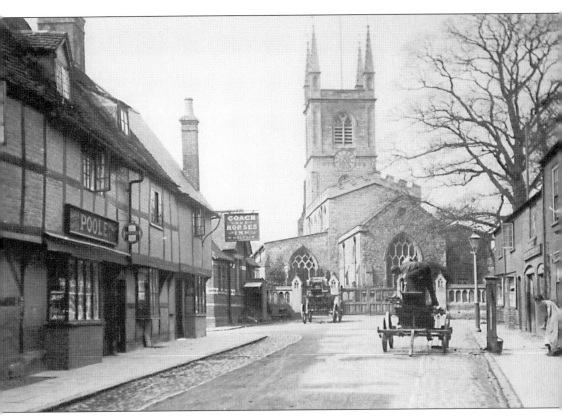

Church Street, c. 1910. The fire engine fills up with water at the pump; the fire station was situated at the rear of the Mechanics Institute which is the building behind the Coach and Horses sign. Traders visible in this view are, on the left, Poole's pies and cakes, William Holyoak at the pub and, opposite, Carters the carpenters.

Kings Head public house, pictured just before demolition in the late 1950s. The first large window was Wormleighton's greengrocer shop. These buildings are situated on the site of the present day car park with the Kings Head door facing the town hall door.

Mrs Webb's Grocers and provision merchant. The proprietor stands outside her shop in Bell Street talking to Mrs Wormleighton. Mrs Smith stands behind carrying a very large basket.

Spital Mill, c. 1910. Children are playing in the millstream. The wooden bridge spanned the river in between the mill and the mill race.

Cottages in Regent Street. A row of empty cottages is pictured in 1968 shortly before their demolition. The building on the far right used to be The Peacock public house, which closed in 1900. The archway led to one of the several different yards that used to exist in Lutterworth, named, of course, Peacock's yard. In their place Regents Court flats were built, completed in 1971.

This is the famous first jet aeroplane engine built by Sir Frank Whittle. The Whittle engine W1 after its second re-build is seen here on test in the original test building in Lutterworth on 10 October 1938. The first flight engine the W1X was also built and tested at Lutterworth and is now on display in the Smithsonian Museum in America.

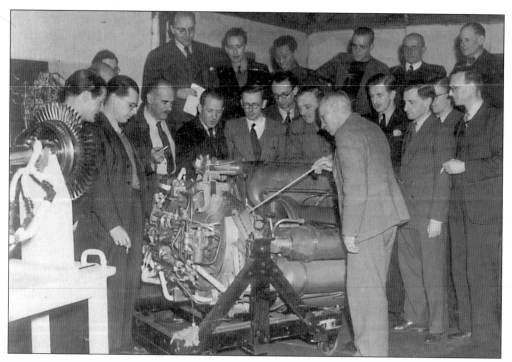

The Power Jets training school. This was opened and run at the Ladywood works in Lutterworth. Here you can see Mr Frank Boston demonstrating the workings of a W2/500 engine to a group of engineers. The training school continued at Ladywood works until 1945.

E28/39; the first successful jet aircraft. This picture was quite a find as it was taken outside the Robin hanger at Farnborough in 1942; this being a top secret establishment during wartime it was not the sort of place anyone should have been taking photographs. A full size copy of this aircraft has been made by the Sir Frank Whittle Commemoration group and is to be placed on the island near to the M1 junction 20.

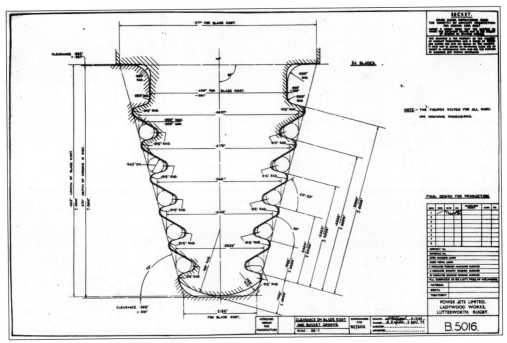

Original plans. This is one of the original plans drawn at the Ladywood Works in Lutterworth in 1942 for the fir tree root system developed by Sir Frank Whittle for holding a turbine blade turning at very high speed. This system is still widely used today.

The station, seen here around 1958, opened on 15 March 1899 and was part of the Great Central, later LNER then BR. It was closed as part of Beeching's cuts on 3 May 1969. The station goods yard has now been transformed into a housing estate.

The view from the station. On occasions when people were late and seen rushing down Station Road, the guard who would have been standing on the station bridge could see them in the distance and would hold the train to enable them to catch it. Station Road prior to the arrival of the station was known as Ely Lane.

Feilding Palmer Hospital and Court House, Lutterworth

Gilmorton Road, *c.* 1910. In the distance, on the right, can be seen the Magistrates Court, which opened in 1906. The court and adjoining police house were erected at a total cost of £3,100. Previously the court had been held at the town hall. Its use as a courthouse was discontinued in 1998 and although it was a Community Building, it was sold by Leicestershire County Council to a private buyer!

Feast Week parade. 'Disarm the Women's Institute', states the placard. The cottages in the background are where the library now stands.

The High School netball team, 1946. From left to right, back row: Yvonne Payne, Doris Phillips, Enid Barnett, Iris Brown, Greta Taylor, Eva Wilson. Front row: Sonia Hill, Betty Lee, Daphne Hancock.

Sports on the school field. The race finishes at the High School with Zillah Mawby in first place, Eileen Bray second and Dolly Smith coming in third.

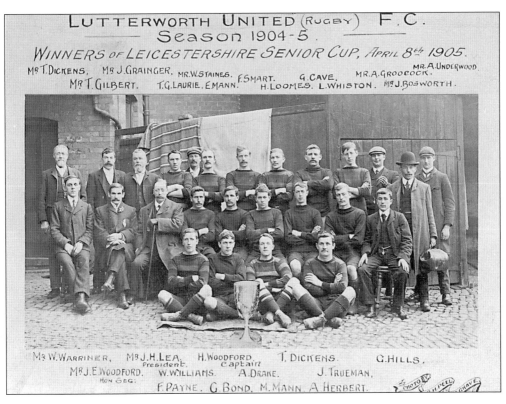

Lutterworth United, 1904.

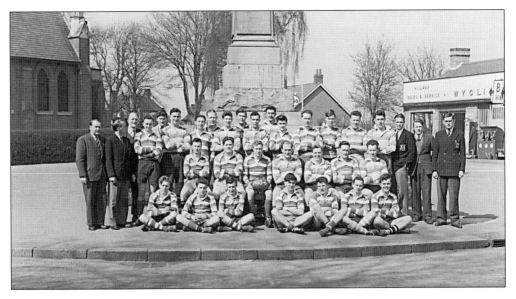

Lutterworth rugby team at the monument, 1955/56.

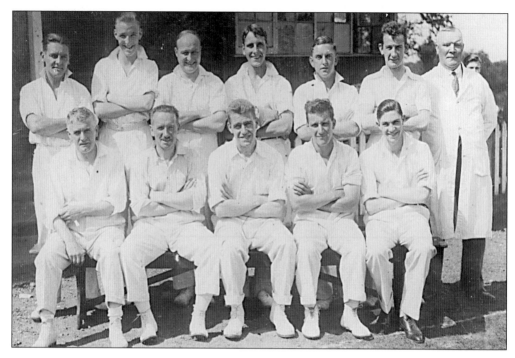

The cricket club. A group of Lutterworth cricketers including Jack Woodford, Reg Hudson, Joe Burgess, John Chapman, George Bond, Frank Wheeler, Henry Dickenson and Walt Laughton.

The bowls club, c. 1960. Standing from left to right: Jack ?, Jock Stein, -?-, -?-, Wilf Lill, Cyril ?, Walter Barrs, -?-, Baz Holdsworth, Frank Clarke, Graham Pearcey, -?-, -?-, John Smith, Harry Butler, Frank Woodward, -?-. Front. Brian Butler, -?-, Sam Dyson (captain), -?-, Les Tilley.

Stoney Hollow, *c.* 1895. Looking down cobbled Stoney Hollow with the conker tree and water pump in the centre and Regent Street on the left. The cobbles are still there today thanks to the efforts of local resident Mrs Joan Page, who campaigned against their removal.

Regent Street. These cottages were knocked down in the 1930s and replaced with Jubilee Cottages in 1935.

A house in Regent Street. Over a period of 100 years this building has also been a private residence, several different shops, jailhouse and police house. When the cage that was used to hold prisoners was filled in, a penny whistle was found at the back that had belonged to one of the prisoners, It is now on display at the museum along with other related items.

Co-operative Society staff at the Bitteswell Road shop pose in the doorway in 1914. Look how beautifully they have arranged the large selection of soaps and soap powders in the right hand window.

The Silver Jubilee celebrations for King George V began with a fancy dress parade through the town, 6 May 1935.

The gas showrooms in Station Road were decorated, as were many other businesses in the town, for the Jubilee of King George V and Queen Mary, 1935.

Crowds gather at the monument. 'The parade ended at the monument where local builder Peter Rourke gave an address to the crowds. It was then onto the Cherry Orchard for an afternoon of sports followed by tea at 4.30 p.m.'

51

The Wheeler family sitting on the gate at the entrance to Spital Mill. Joe and Frank are joined by two of their relatives.

The crowning of the May Queen. A large crowd gathers in Coventry Road to watch this annual event. If you were to take a photograph today from the same position you would be looking into the library windows.

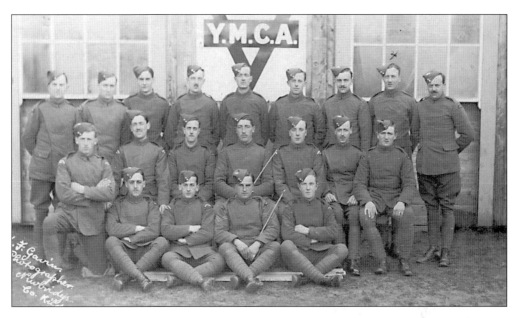

Soldiers outside the YMCA in Market Street, 1916. This building was also the office of Peter Rourke, a local builder.

The Vedonis factory always took part in the annual event by entering a float in the parade.

Born in Nottinghamshire in 1846, George Spencer moved to Lutterworth in 1902 and set up in business with the Barrowcliffe brothers in a factory in New Street making knitted textiles. The business failed and in 1908 George set up G. Spencer & Co. in Crescent Road. This business succeeded and the company moved to larger premises specially built on the Leicester Road known as the Vedonis works. George Spencer became a generous benefactor to Lutterworth. He gave land to the Cottage Hospital, money towards a clean water supply, £5,000 in 1939 for the maternity and isolation wings at the hospital and the district nurses house. He also gave the recreation ground to the Parish Council and the cricket club to the Town Estate Trustees. He is remembered in Lutterworth by the road named after him and by the Spencer Rooms in Market Street.

George Spencer's workers, c. 1914. Mr Spencer was well known for treating his employees to a day out at the coast, including meals and an ice cream.

Ray Walker's dance band. Ray Walker was well known in the area. He built his own cars, motorcycles and cycles (The Denbigh A1). He had a garage in Bank Street, then Market Street where he also gave music lessons to the children of the town.

An original poster advertising the band.

MEMORIAL HALL
CLAYBROOKE.

DANCE

TO BE HELD ON

Wednesday, March 14th

From 8.30 p.m. prompt till 11.30 p.m.

RAY WALKER'S BAND

Proceeds for Claybrooke Local Forces Fund

No admittance under fourteen years

REFRESHMENTS AT
MODERATE PRICES.

ADMISSION: 2/- ; FORCES 1/6

The VAD (Voluntary Aid Detachment) hospital was set up in a schoolroom in the Methodist chapel in 1915. Under the guidance of Nurse Britton, from the Cottage Hospital, 30 volunteers tended the wounded; the 20 beds were rarely empty. A total of 539 men were treated during the three years it was open. The first patients were admitted in April 1915. The inscription on the back of this photograph reads: 'Last photo taken at the VAD hospital 7 November 1918, closed 9 November 1918.'

Cottages in Regent Street. The building on the left was formerly the police officer's house. Below the railings and underneath the road was the 'cage' or prison cell.

Lutterworth Rural District Council, 1961. From left to right, back row: H. Drake, R. Baker, W. Attfield, Dr A. Ross, J. Bown, J. Wright, J. O'Reynolds. Middle row: H. McNaught, F. Shaw, Revd Proctor, Revd Batten, F. Howkins, W. Smyth, B. Mcquillin, W. Cooke, E. Ford, R. Hounsfield, A. Wood, E. Herbert, R. Durran, H. Sims, J. Cooper. Front row: A. Notley, T. Stevens, C. Bray, G. Bassett, L. Pickering, A. Ashton, C. Hill, E. Illson, L.Tanner.

The workhouse opened in 1840 to house 200 inmates taken from the previous building, thought to have been in the town centre, and the workhouse at Ullesthorpe. It was designed by Mr (later Sir) Gilbert Scott. It ceased functioning as a workhouse in 1948 but continued as a home for the elderly until its demolition in 1970 when it was replaced with the current building.

Station Road, with The White Hart Inn on the left. When the cottage on the right was demolished, Mr Bernard Laughton who lived next door remembers that everyone was covered in fleas which apparently came from the thatch.

Lutterworth Womens Institute. The Lutterworth branch of the institute began in 1930. This occasion was its twenty-first birthday party.

L. Jones, Church Street. This was a very busy newsagents and toyshop in the town centre for many years.

Barnaby Rudge, landlord of the Denbigh Arms. This amusing advertisement for the hotel was taken from *Bottrill's Almanack* in 1914.

BARNABY RUDGE is dead it is said
To regions above or below he has fled,
Do not believe it but just call, I pray,
At the 'Denbigh Arms,' Lutterworth way.

For there you will find him all blithesome and gay
The same jovial landlord day after day,
And though to the 'Denbigh' you may have to trudge
You'll never regret seeing Barnaby Rudge.

BARNABY RUDGE.
Not from 'Dickens' but late of the 'Leicestershire's.'

THE "DENBIGH"

First-Class Family & Commercial Hotel
LUTTERWORTH.

LARGEST IN THE DISTRICT.
Billiards, Coffee, and Private Sitting Rooms.
EVERY ACCOMMODATION FOR LARGE
OR SMALL PARTIES.

Posting in all its Branches. :: :: Good Stabling for Hunters,
GARAGE. INSPECTION PIT.
Expert Mechanics at Hand.
Headquarters—C.T.C.

PROPRIETOR - BARNABY RUDGE.

Wycliffe Garage. At this time the three star petrol on the right was 6s 4d a gallon. The garage has now moved to the Leicester Road.

Kimpton Smith's, High Street. This shop moved around over the years having started life in the old shop at the side of the National Westminster Bank then moving to the shop over the road as in the picture then moving to the building next to the town hall.

George Street. This is now the entrance to the Co-op. This view shows the house and small shop belonging to Mr Buck the brewer. Miss Gold from Bitteswell worked in the shop for many years.

M. Salter painted this watercolour of Buck's Brewery in 1993. The brewery, which was run by the Buck family, was of such high quality that it was only one of two to be allowed to bottle Guinness for the company outside Ireland.

The Atherstone hunt are pictured outside the Board Inn, High Street, 3 March 1905.

A group in fancy dress, 1938. We know the date as it is embroidered on a lady's hat, second row, third from the left. Included in the picture are: Jessie Withers, Mrs Dutton, Miss Blunt, Mrs Buck, Mrs Underwood, Doris Bonsor, Mrs Langham, Mrs McCloud, Enid Bonsor, Nellie Lewin, Mrs Fletcher, Mrs Small, Mrs Beryl, Annie Smith, Rita Tailby, Joyce Robinson, Amy Holland, Mrs Marchant, and Ada Holland.

Land Army girls in a parade passing by the Ram Inn.

Broadside Burton. Ex-England
speedway captain, JP, and garage
owner, Mr Squib Burton is pictured
with some of his trophies.

Hotpoint fire, 1976. A plume of billowing smoke fills the sky as the Hotpoint factory burns. The fire destroyed the factory and the company had to relocate to Peterborough.

Peace procession, 1919. This was held on the agricultural showground on the Leicester Road. First prize to went Mr Bond with Annie Duffus as driver.

Bitteswell Road, c. 1930. The very wide verge makes this picture hard to recognize, it appears to be wider than the road itself.

Accident outside the Springs. On a wet day an army lorry towing a bowser was hit by a coal lorry coming down High Street. The resulting collision demolished the wall at the Spring's but fortunately no one was injured.

High Street with the town's market on both sides of the street, *c.* 1910. A wonderful old lamp hangs outside the Board Inn.

Staff at the Raleigh works. The Vedonis building was used by Raleigh and Rover during the war, making shell cases for the war effort.

Opposite, top: The playing fields were at the rear of the original Grammar School building. *Bottom:* Cottages opposite the mechanics institute. These were pulled down and replaced by the Baker Street Flats.

W. T. NURDEN,

THE DAIRY.

GEORGE STREET,

LUTTERWORTH. ::

ALL KINDS OF CHOCOLATES AND CONFECTIONERY IN STOCK.

NEW LAID EGGS,

DRESSED POULTRY,

AND

FARM BUTTER.

A TRIAL SOLICITED.

—ALL MILK SOLD—

MORNING AND EVENING

GUARANTEED NEW.

Let me Bottle some for you.

Cream Ices, Wholesale & Retail.

Nurdens Delivery Van. Mr and Mrs Nurden ran their shop in George Street selling sweets and ice creams. They took over the business in the early 1930s and continued trading for over thirty years.

An advertisement from *Bottrill's Almanack* 1934.

Clarke's butchers. This building was The Bell Inn public house from the end of the 1700s for approximately forty years. It then became a butcher's shop and private residence until, after restoration work, it re-opened in 1984 as the Shambles public house.

Opening of Clarke's butchers shop.

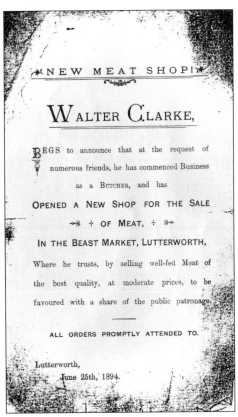

★ N E W   M E A T   S H O P! ★

WALTER CLARKE,

BEGS to announce that at the request of numerous friends, he has commenced Business as a BUTCHER, and has

OPENED A NEW SHOP FOR THE SALE

→* ÷ OF MEAT, ÷ *←

IN THE BEAST MARKET, LUTTERWORTH,

Where he trusts, by selling well-fed Meat of the best quality, at moderate prices, to be favoured with a share of the public patronage.

ALL ORDERS PROMPTLY ATTENDED TO.

Lutterworth,
June 25th, 1894.

1st Lutterworth Cub Scouts pictured at their headquarters with leader Charlie Robinson.

Town band, 1910. Included in the photograph are, from left to right: W. Wormleighton, H. Spriggs, T. Bosworth, R. Shipman, F. Rose, J. Payne. H. Bosworth, S. Poole, J. Wheeler, A. Wheeler, J. Gilbert, J. Herbert, F. Herbert, T. Busby, T. Smith.

Accident on High Street. A lorry carrying large rolls of paper shed its load in High Street causing a problem for the local police. The chaos was exacerbated because Regent Street was being demolished at that time.

A Coronation celebrations party is held in the church hall in 1953 and everyone is enjoying the day.

Coventry Road. All looks quiet on the Coventry Road but under closer scrutiny, in the distance, we find a tradesman selling his wares, three men watching a cricket match from the roadside and a two-seater Morris Cowley is parked opposite the cricket ground.

Coronation Day parade, 1911. The children pass by Chesterfield's grocery shop in Church Street on the way around the town.

High Street, *c*. 1950. Before the town centre car park was built the market was held on the pavement either side of High Street.

High school teachers: Mr White, Miss Peace, Miss Pearce, Mr Lovett (Billy), -?-.

The Narrows. Standing outside the Greyhound Inn we can see the demolition of the town centre buildings. Kimpton Smith's, Morris the butchers, Buswells chemist and a three-storey house disappeared. Looking down the street you can see why it was called the Narrows.

Greyhound yard, the rear of the pub in the 1960s. At one time two large concrete drums were kept in the yard. These were to be rolled out into High Street, filled with concrete, for use as tank traps during the Second World War.

Town centre. The road was widened and the space made by the demolition of the tall shops and private houses, making way for the town centre car park/market square that we have today.

A party was held at Hardings in 1957 or 1958 to celebrate several of the employees twenty-five years service with this well known local building company. From left to right, back row: Arthur Barlow, Alan Brough, Bill Granger, Tim Hensman, Cliff Cobley, Bill Whitworth, Brian Green, Hubert Herbert, Bill Green, Alan Hinson, Eric Dickens, George Bingham, Jim Taylor, Fred Timson. Centre row: Bill Worledge, John Fox, -?-, Mrs Hensman, Mrs Herbert, Mrs Whitworth, Mrs Green, Mrs Granger, Mrs Bingham, Mrs Taylor, Mrs Timson, Mrs Brough, -?-. Front row: Mrs Worledge, The Earl and Countess of Denbigh, Mr and Mrs Harding, Bill Jackson, Mrs Jackson.

King's coal merchants. Next to Mr Burrows' off licence and taxi business stands the coal storehouse. In the front of this building were two very old windows both of overlapping bulls-eye type.

The Wycliffe charabanc. A real occasion for a group of Lutterworth ladies in the 1920s, as they get ready for an outing in the Wycliffe charabanc. Mrs Creaser is standing by the door with Joan Busby, Mrs Eagle and Mrs Earl from the fish shop sit behind.

Church Street at the turn of the last century. Just past the children on the right is the shop of F.J. Banbury, fishmonger, on the corner of Bank Street is the Unicorn Inn before it was demolished and re-built. On the opposite corner is Bank House a music school run by Miss Bottrill.

Demolition of the council offices. The council offices had previously relocated to Lutterworth House, Woodmarket, and the building had been a private residence for some years.

Fire at the cricket club. A Lutterworth fire fighter tries to quench the flames. Built in 1938 the famous cricket pavilion was totally destroyed in an arson attack.

New cricket club opening, 3 May 1998. A proud day for Lutterworth. After a massive fund raising effort, the Lutterworth Cricket Club holds its official opening ceremony.

Cottage hospital. The Feilding-Palmer cottage hospital opened in 1900 and is named after the family who were the Lords of the Manor. Mrs Feilding-Palmer donated the ground where the hospital is built in memory of her late husband. Many generous bequests were left to the hospital in the years following its opening enabling it to expand.

Mills family in 1914. The family were a group of travelling performers who regularly put on shows for the people of Lutterworth and local villages.

Interior of St Mary's church. At one time all of the facing walls were painted as you can see in the picture, but over the years much of the painting has been covered over.

Rectory gardens. The annual church fête was held in these gardens for many years. After the new rectory was built this building was converted into sheltered housing for the elderly.

LUTTERWORTH RECTORY · J. ABBOTT. PHOTO.

Church Street after a heavy snowfall – the paths have been cleared onto the road. This would not pose such a problem for horses as it would have done in later years for cars.

Church Street 1897. The Rainbow brothers and their dog join in the celebrations to mark Queen Victoria's Diamond Jubilee.

Station Road. Lutterworth station with the milk dray approaching the bridge. You can just see a man in the gateway. This was the entrance to Wormleighton's market garden.

The Meeting House, the United Reformed church, built in 1777. This picture is from an etching dating from around 1800.

Air Training Corps. The 1269 Lutterworth and Broughton Astley Squadrons of the ATC at RAF Bobbington (Halfpenny Green) in 1940 standing in front of an Avro Anson.

Feast Week float. The parade travels down Woodway Road into Woodmarket. In the background you can see the buildings of the former workhouse.

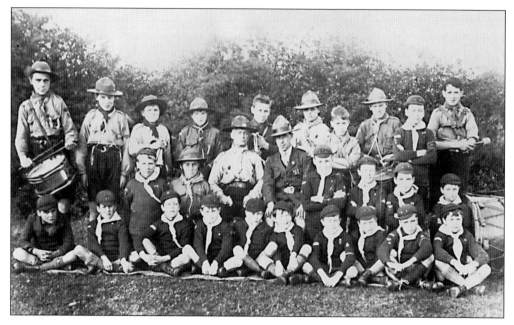

Lutterworth Scouts line up for an early photograph with their drummers.

The wedding in Lutterworth of Gertrude Corrall and Edward Croft on 17 September 1902. From left to right: Alicia Petch, Annie Croft, Edward Croft, Hayes Petch, Gertrude Corrall, Emma Corrall, George Corrall. The Corrall family were clockmakers in Lutterworth from 1725 to 1867.

An accident in High Street, c. 1968. A Euclid earthmover working on the excavations for the M1 crashed into Sketchley's dry cleaners window. Fortunately no one was hurt.

St John's Ambulance Parade. Crowds gather outside St John's Hall. One of the St Johns volunteers from this area was Mr Ray Binley who you would often find with his camera filming anything that was going on in the town.

Lutterworth Mothers Union, c. 1920. The gentleman in the centre of the front row is Canon Hindley who was vicar of St Mary's from 1918 to 1926.

Group at the waterfall on the River Swift in between Misterton and Lutterworth. From left to right: Francis Voss, Ida Herbert, Ivy Williams, Anne Robinson. The waterfall and the Big Boys Bathey (a deep part on a bend in the river) were well-used recreation facilities by the youngsters of the town.

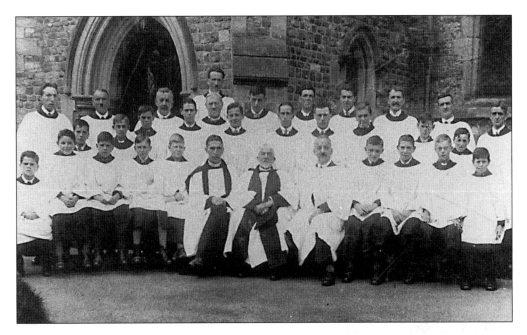

Choir, *c.* 1924. From left to right, back row: Walter Allso, William Buck, Charlie Haswell, John Kimpton-Smith, Tom Bromley, Ted Jary, Bert Green, Amos Ward, Bert Crooke. Middle row: John Chapman, Ron Pearson, Lance Barrs, Tommy Wells, Chris Grainger, Ted Drake, George Keeling, Sam Wood, Cyril Hancock, Eric Wells, Bert Illiffe. Front row: Reg Granger, Wally Wells, Jack Bolland, George Beck, Frank Peat, Revd M.L. Hunt (curate), Canon Paton Hindley, George Haswell (choirmaster), Noel Nash, Henry Coleman, Frank Barrs, Joe Bozeat. At the very back on his own is Frank Wheeler.

Choir and bell ringer's dinner. A few years later a dinner for the choir and bell ringers was attended by many of the choir members pictured above.

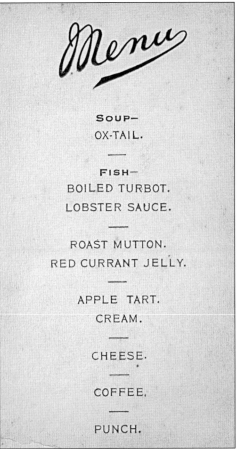

Menu

SOUP—
OX-TAIL.

—

FISH—
BOILED TURBOT.
LOBSTER SAUCE.

—

ROAST MUTTON.
RED CURRANT JELLY.

—

APPLE TART.
CREAM.

—

CHEESE.

—

COFFEE.

—

PUNCH.

The Revd Champness retired to Lutterworth in 1901 and settled in a house in Station Road. He preached in the overcrowded chapel and it was this that made him decide to take on the task of raising money to build a new one. In an amazingly short space of time funds were raised to enable the building to be started. The total cost was to be £2,600.

The Wycliffe Memorial Methodist church. One year later on 25 April 1905 the church opened its doors for the first time. Revd Champness preached the sermon, and the proceeds for the day reached the sum of £560. One year later the church was completely paid for, a magnificent achievement. The whole project from the Revd Champness's first idea to completion took a little over $2\frac{1}{2}$ years. Sadly he did not live to celebrate the first anniversary, as he passed away after a short illness in October 1905.

Wesleyan Church, Lutterworth

Crowds arriving for the opening ceremony of the Methodist church.

Children gather for a Punch and Judy show on the foundry field. The Follsain Wycliffe gala day was an annual event on the Leicester road field.

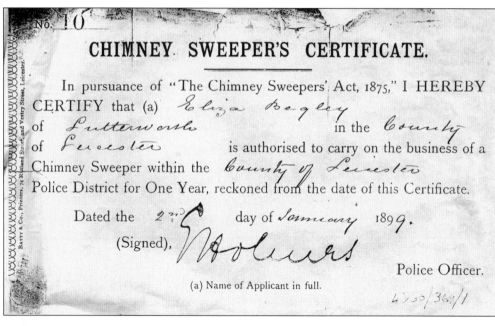

No. 10

CHIMNEY SWEEPER'S CERTIFICATE.

In pursuance of "The Chimney Sweepers' Act, 1875," I HEREBY CERTIFY that (a) *Eliza Begley* of *Lutterworth* in the *County* of *Leicester* is authorised to carry on the business of a Chimney Sweeper within the *County of Leicester* Police District for One Year, reckoned from the date of this Certificate.

Dated the 2nd day of *January* 1899.

(Signed), *Holmes*

Police Officer.

(a) Name of Applicant in full.

4250/369/1

Eliza and Sam Begley were both authorised chimney sweeps.

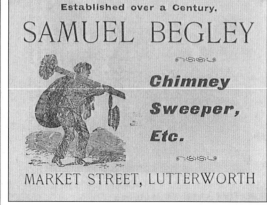

Established over a Century.

SAMUEL BEGLEY

Chimney Sweeper, Etc.

MARKET STREET, LUTTERWORTH

Left: Sam and Eliza Begley ran a chimney sweep business in Lutterworth. The business traded for over 100 years as can be seen in the advertisement taken from *Abbott's Almanac* in 1907.

Above: Advertisement from *Abbott's Almanack*, 1907.

90

Regent Street viewed at the turn of the last century. Two horse-drawn carts come in from Woodmarket passing the conker tree and the right hand turning into Stoney Hollow. The houses on the left were demolished to make way for the new Stoney Hollow road layout and those on the right to make way for Jubilee cottages.

Bank Street, 1906. The horse and cart stand outside the cinema. The sign on the right for Walker's motor shop which is now a hairdressers can just be seen.

Coronation day, 2 June 1953. The choir leads the way to the war memorial where a service was held. The church bells rang out at regular intervals throughout the day. In the afternoon street parties were held and the children were each given a coronation beaker.

High Street, 2 June 1953. The celebrations continued, starting in the evening at 6 p.m. on the recreation ground with dancing displays, sports and a motorcycle riding display by Squib Burton and Reg Cheney. The evening finished with a bonfire and firework display.

Church Street. There has not been a lot of change in this street in the last 100 years with the notable exception of the tree, which had dominated the scene for so long but sadly had to be felled for safety reasons due to disease.

Station Road, 1906. A good view showing the width of the road at the top and some of the wonderful thatched houses that are no longer in existence.

Bank Street. Looking up the street the 'Drovers' cottages are on the right. Drovers were people who would walk farm animals from one town or village to the next, taking them to market or moving them for grazing.

W.A. Dalzells Great Central Supply Stores. Mr Dalzell opened his shop in 1896, he continued in business for the next forty-six years.

An advertisement for Mr Green's plumbing business in 1906 from *Bottrill's Almanack.*

Mr Green and his associates putting up the first windmill in the district, just off the Leicester Road. The mills were used by farmers to raise water up from a well situated beneath. On the right is Mr John Granger and the man standing lower down in the windmill tower is Mr Ernie Granger.

High Street, *c.* 1860. A Victorian street scene is captured in an etching by an unknown artist.

Hobley's Refreshment Room's. Later these would become Johnsons Tea Rooms.

Unveiling ceremony of the war memorial. Crowds gather to watch the unveiling ceremony on 24 May 1921. Those attending included ex-servicemen, relatives of those killed in the war,

members of the VAD, cadets, the town band, choir, boy scouts and school children. Members of the public were allowed to view the memorial after the ceremony had taken place.

Jesus Drake, the proprietor, stands outside his premises on the corner of Church Street and Bank Street. Advertised on the wall to the left of his head is an unusual item – he sold Lutterworth lettered rock!

The Shambles, Bell Street. This is shortly before building renovations were undertaken by Ned and Kelly Allen.

Lutterworth Brownies, 1924/25.

The Welfare group in the grounds of the grammar school in 1937.

John and Mrs Dickenson, dressed as Pearly King and Queen, walk down Bitteswell Road in another Feast Week parade.

In later years the Collins Coach Works building was transformed into the Lutterworth Garage and Motor Works, run by Mr Claude Grewcock. The building was later demolished and this site is now the entrance into the Co-op.

Mr Albert Holland and his dog, Hennessey, 1958. Holland's funfair has been coming to the town for many years and has always been a very exciting time. The dodgems, helter skelter, cyclone, and many stalls kept the children amused and became *the* meeting place over the weeks that it stayed.

A typical Sunday at the 'Swift' with everyone in their best clothes.

The sailing ship *Lutterworth* in Nelson harbour, New Zealand. This was a barque of 883 tons, launched from Hartlepool in 1868 and was purchased by the Shaw Savill Company for the New Zealand trade. After sailing between New Zealand and England for thirty years she was sold to Turnbull & Co.

A few months after being sold the ship was de-masted in a gale in the Cooks Straight. Later the ship went aground in Nelson Harbour (where this picture was taken) and was later scrapped.

Nine
Peatling Parva

Main Street, c. 1900. This shows the extent of the village at that time, the only part not seen is the cottages near the Hall entrance, the Hall itself and the church.

Mr Moore watches his wife take the photographs as he sits on the remains of the mud walls from an old building demolished long ago.

The Laurels, pictured by Mrs Moore of Queens Road, Clarendon Park, Leicester, c. 1905. Mrs Moore was one of the most important local photographers of her time, granting us the opportunity to see some wonderful images of Edwardian life.

The church and rectory. St Andrews church, which shows traces of thirteenth-century elements, was restored in 1876 still with an original nave roof.

The Manor House used to be situated next to the church but was demolished early in the last century.

Main Street. Three workhorses are taken along the street by the farm hands, ready for another day's work in the fields. Mr Stephen Lee's butchers shop was just past the inn on the right.

Main Street. The school children of the village, dressed in their smocks, come to see what's going on. (Vanished Views)

Ten
Shawell

Shawell Feast was an annual event and the carousel from the Twigden family of Dunton Bassett was the same one used in the Goose Fair in Nottingham at the turn of the last century.

Weslyan church. This unusual corrugated tin structure still stands today, a testimony to the original workmanship.

The children knew to stand perfectly still to allow the photographer to capture this picture outside their house, Shawell, in early 1900s.

Standing by the bridge are thirteen of the village's children, all very well turned out, hats on and in their best Sunday clothes. The road over the bridge leads to Swinford from the Gibbet Island. The houses off to the right are on the road to Cathorpe and the A5.

Shawell school. This school is now a private residence but still retains the school bell in its original position.

The White Swan. The landlord Mr Charles Binnersley and his family look out from what was a very large public house for such a small village. This pub advertised on its outside wall a 'Tea and Refreshment Room'. The main door has recently been re-opened.

The old cottages. Shawell has a stream and allotments in the centre of the village and with many of the buildings being of different design; a wonderful Victorian feel is retained.

Eleven
North and South Kilworth

Across the green. This shows the back way into the school. (Vanished Views)

The large house on the South Kilworth to Stanford road, later to be modified to the Monte Bello of today. (Vanished Views)

South Kilworth shop. The advertising signs stand outside the village shop. (Vanished Views)

The office staff. Mr Webb took this picture of A. Staines, W.H. Higham, ? Watts, and F.L. Grindle. This could be a South Kilworth company or perhaps the railway office?

North Kilworth. Back Lane is pictured, with the old mud wall on the right.

The Memorial Hall. At the top you can just see the spire of St Andrews church.

The old part of the village. A very muddy road leads to the main part of the village in this sleepy, virtually untouched part of the county.

Twelve
Ullesthorpe

Ullesthorpe Court. A house has stood on this site since 1767 and is the former home of the Goodacre family. This impressive building was formerly known as Four Elms, it has also been used as a museum, and a VAD (Voluntary Aid Detachment) Hospital for twenty sick and wounded soldiers during the First World War. It is now a hotel and sports complex.

Two-up and two-down. An early picture of a small cottage in the village in the 1890s.

Cottage industry. This is the same cottage, which is now being used by Mr C. Burley as a boot and shoe shop.

The Engine public house stood on the approach road to Ullesthorpe railway station. (Vanished Views)

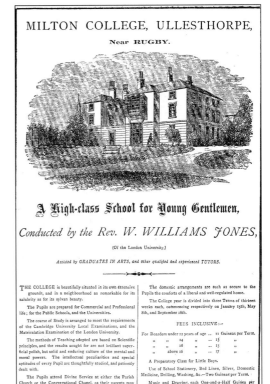

MILTON COLLEGE, ULLESTHORPE,

Near RUGBY.

A High-class School for Young Gentlemen,

Conducted by the Rev. W. WILLIAMS JONES,

(Of the London University,)

Assisted by GRADUATES IN ARTS, and other qualified and experienced TUTORS.

THE COLLEGE is beautifully situated in its own extensive grounds; and in a neighbourhood as remarkable for its salubrity as for its sylvan beauty.

The Pupils are prepared for Commercial and Professional life; for the Public Schools, and the Universities.

The course of Study is arranged to meet the requirements of the Cambridge University Local Examinations, and the Matriculation Examination of the London University.

The methods of Teaching adopted are based on Scientific principles, and the results sought for are not brilliant superficial polish, but solid and enduring culture of the mental and moral powers. The intellectual peculiarities and special aptitudes of every Pupil are thoughtfully studied, and patiently dealt with.

The Pupils attend Divine Service at either the Parish Church or the Congregational Chapel, as their parents may desire

The domestic arrangements are such as secure to the Pupils the comforts of a liberal and well-regulated home.

The College year is divided into three Terms of thirteen weeks each, commencing respectively on January 15th, May 8th, and September 18th.

FEES INCLUSIVE:—

For Boarders under 12 years of age .. 11 Guineas per Term.
    „   „   14 „ .. 13   „
    „   „   16 „ .. 15   „
    „ above 16 „ .. 17   „

A Preparatory Class for Little Boys.

Use of School Stationery, Bed Linen, Silver, Domestic Medicine, Drilling, Washing, &c.—Two Guineas per Term.

Music and Drawing, each One-and-a-Half Guinea per Term extra.

An advertisement for a school found in the back of Whites Directory of Leicestershire 1877.

The Congregational chapel. Built in 1825 this two-storey building has arched windows and a hipped roof. Past the chapel on the left is the manse and further up on the right is the old post office.

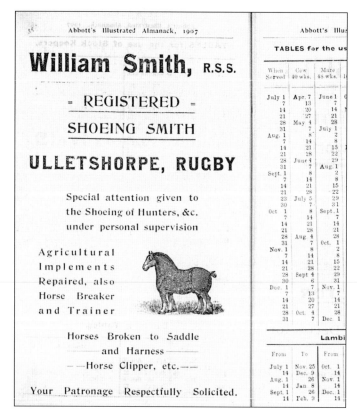

Advertisment for William Smith. This is taken from *Abbott's Almanack* of 1907 and includes an original printing error!

Thirteen
Walcote

The Red Lion pub was sold along with its brew house in 1810 by Mr Thomas Cooper, a carpenter and joiner. It was on the left hand side as you go into Walcote from Lutterworth. By 1898 it was owned by Northampton's Lion Brewery, and later it was sold again and demolished. The sign also advertises the fact that 'Good Stabling' was on offer, as it was at many of the public houses at that time.

A trip out for the men. From left to tight: Richard Bray, Mr Henslow, Teddy Masters (on the bus), William Bray, Arch Curtis, Jack Baylis (publican), Jack Bray, Jack Bray junior, -?-, Joe Cooke, James Bray, George Horsewood, Walter Voss, Ted Neale.

This building stood on the corner of the South Kilworth/Market Harborough turn in the early 1900s.

This unusual thatched farmhouse has evolved over many years, having been considerably changed, with extensions added, and windows and doors altered or filled in. The young girl at the gate is walking towards the bridge over the stream in the bottom of the picture. A pistol dating from around 1890 was found in this stream a few years ago and is now on display in the museum.

A member of the Green family of Walcote presents a cup to Miss Eileen Bray.

The Black Horse. A horse and trap leaves the inn with Mrs Morris at the reins. The Morris family were publicans in the village for many years.

Mr Linden. This man should have been very famous. He lived in Walcote and worked in Lutterworth and was the inventor of the football bladder, for keeping footballs inflated. His wife, it is said, died because of this as she used to inflate the pigs bladders that were being used in his experiments; in doing so tragically caught a fatal disease.

Fourteen
Other Local Villages

Walton Cricket Club. Winners of the Lutterworth and District League 1926 Challenge Cup and Aikman Cup. The photograph was taken outside Walton Hall.

Kimcote and Walton school, 1923.

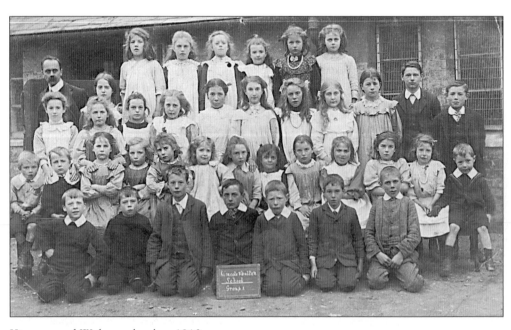

Kimcote and Walton school, *c.* 1910.

Ashby Magna post office, situated next to the village hall was the only shop in the area.

In the distance you can see the topiary work outside the post office.

Highly decorative railings surround this eighteenth-century farmhouse in a sleepy corner of the village of Bruntingthorpe.

The old rectory, Frolesworth, was an imposing structure with stuccoed frontage and irregularly gabled sides. The wrought-iron gates are of eighteenth-century origin.